LIVING WELL

PERSONAL

HYGIENE

AND GOOD HEALTH

by Shirley Wimbish Gray

THE CHILD'S WORLD®

CHANHASSEN, MINNESOTA

Published in the United States of America by The Child's World®
P.O. Box 326, Chanhassen, MN 55317-0326
800-599-READ
www.childsworld.com

Subject Consultant:
Diana Ruschhaupt,
Director of Programs,
Ruth Lilly Health
Education Center,
Indianapolis,
Indianapolis

Photo Credits: Cover: Creatas; Corbis: 6 (Lester V. Bergman), 8 (Nancy Ney), 9 (Michael Prince), 10 (Chris Collins), 13 (Jose Luis Pelaez, Inc.), 14 (Andrew Brookes), 15 (James Noble), 18 right (Jim Zuckerman), 19 (NASA/Roger Ressmeyer), 22 (George Contorakes), 23, 24 (Cynthia Hart Designer), 26 (Lowell Georgia), 27 (David Pollack), 28, 31; Corbis Sygma: 7 (Baumgartner Olivia), 18 (Parrot Pascal), 21; Custom Medical Stock Photo: 11, 11 right, 12, 15 right, 16, 17; PhotoEdit: 5 (David Young-Wolff), 20 (Mary Kate Denny), 21 right (Myrleen Ferguson Cate), 25 (Michael Newman).

The Child's World®: Mary Berendes, Publishing Director

Editorial Directions, Inc.: E. Russell Primm, Editorial Director; Elizabeth K. Martin, Line Editor; Katie Marsico, Assistant Editor; Olivia Nellums, Editorial Assistant; Susan Hindman, Copy Editor; Sarah E. De Capua, Proofreader; Peter Garnham and Chris Simms, Fact Checkers; Tim Griffin/IndexServ, Indexer; Elizabeth K. Martin and Matthew Messbarger, Photo Researchers and Selectors

Library of Congress Cataloging-in-Publication Data
Gray, Shirley W.
Personal hygiene and good health / by Shirley Wimbish Gray.
        p. cm.—(Living well)
Includes index.
Contents: Wash your hands!—Keeping germs away—Open wide!—
Germs that hide—Develop good habits.
  ISBN 1-59296-084-7 (lib. bdg. : alk. paper)
1. Hygiene—Juvenile literature. [1. Hygiene. 2. Cleanliness. 3. Bacteria.]
I. Title. II. Series: Living well (Child's World (Firm))
  RA780.G736 2004
  613'.4—dc21
                            2003006282

TABLE OF CONTENTS

CHAPTER ONE

WASH YOUR HANDS!

Emily runs through the door and calls to her mother, "I'm home from soccer practice! I'm starving! May I have something to eat?"

"Yes, after you wash your hands," her mother says.

Emily opens the refrigerator door and starts looking for a snack. "I'm too hungry to wash. I need to eat something first."

"Your hands are covered in germs," her mother says. "You need them to be clean before you start eating."

Emily heads to the sink and washes her hands with soap and water. When she comes back to the kitchen, her mother has cheese and crackers ready for her.

"See, that didn't take too long," her mother says. "Washing your hands before you eat keeps you from getting sick. You don't want to miss soccer because you're sick."

Washing your hands is part of personal **hygiene.** It is one of the simple things you can do every day to keep yourself healthy. Good personal hygiene will help prevent germs from making your body sick. That way you can keep doing the things you enjoy, like playing soccer or being with your friends.

Emily washes her hands to stop the spread of germs so that she won't get sick.

CHAPTER TWO

WHAT ARE GERMS?

Germs are **organisms** that are so small they can only be seen with a microscope. Bacteria (back-TEER-ee-uh) and viruses (VYE-russ-iz) are types of germs. So are certain types of fungi (FUN-guy) and protozoa (pro-toe-ZOH-uh).

Germs sneak into our bodies without us knowing. For example, when someone with a cold sneezes, thousands of germs fly into the air. A person standing nearby may breathe in the germs.

Many germs are spread through our noses and mouths. If you have to sneeze, make sure to cover your mouth.

That is one way you can catch a cold.

Germs can also be passed by things you touch. If you blow your nose and then touch your desk, you could be leaving germs behind. The next student who touches your desk also touches your germs.

It's easy for germs to be spread when you or someone you know gets sick.

Can you keep these germs from getting into your body? Yes and no. You cannot prevent them all from sneaking in. When germs attack, the body's immune system moves into action. Its job is to get rid of the germs so you will not get sick.

You can prevent many germs from ever getting into your body. This is why personal hygiene is important. Good hygiene keeps the germs away.

A great place to start is with the outside of your body. Think about your skin. It is the largest organ of the body. Its job is to hold your bones, muscles, and other organs together. The skin also protects the inside of the body and helps control the body's temperature.

Your skin protects everything inside your body. It is very important to take care of it. Sunscreen is a good way to keep your skin healthy.

Your skin gets dirty doing its job. Dust, dead cells, and sweat stick to it every day. This makes skin a great place for germs to live. Taking a shower or bath every

Keeping your body clean by taking a bath or shower is a good thing to do each and every day.

day will keep this from happening.

A tiny cut in your skin is an open door to germs. When you get cut or scratched, be sure to wash the area with soap and water. You might also need a bandage to help keep germs out until new skin grows.

CHAPTER THREE

HOW CAN YOU KEEP YOUR MOUTH HEALTHY?

F ew parts of your body do as much for you every day as your mouth and teeth. They help you chew and swallow. They help you sip and gulp. They even help you talk, sing, and smile all through the day. Keeping them healthy is important.

Bacteria are the biggest danger for your mouth. They cause tooth decay. Bacteria grow when they find sugar left over from food on your teeth.

Our mouth and teeth help us to do all kinds of things, such as saying "Ahhhh" and acting goofy!

Once bacteria start eating the sugar, they form a film called

plaque (PLAK). Try running your tongue over the front of

your teeth. Then feel the back. The back may

feel rougher than the smooth fronts of

your teeth. If so, you have found

that plaque is forming on the back

of your teeth.

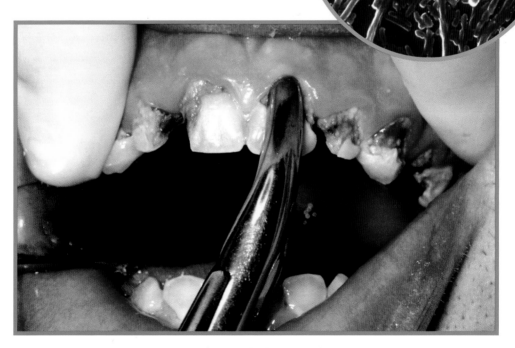

This is what a strain of plaque looks like under a microscope (top).
If you don't take care of your teeth, plaque can build up
until you have to have your dentist remove it (bottom).

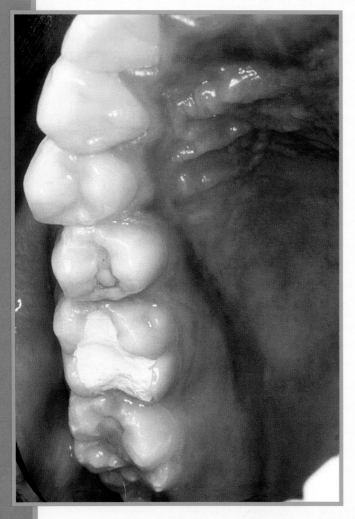

Not taking care of your teeth and gums can result in gingivitis.

Plaque causes several problems for your mouth. It can lead to cavities, or tiny holes in the surface of your teeth. It can also make the gum around your teeth red, swollen, and sore. This is called gingivitis (jin-juh-VI-tis).

Plaque is harmful to your teeth, but it is easy to get rid of. Brushing your teeth twice a day will clean away the sticky mix of sugar and bacteria. Flossing between your teeth once a day removes plaque from the tiny edges of the teeth.

Have you ever noticed that your mouth tastes funny when you wake up in the morning? Dead cells pile up on your tongue and gums during the night when your mouth is dry. Bacteria begin

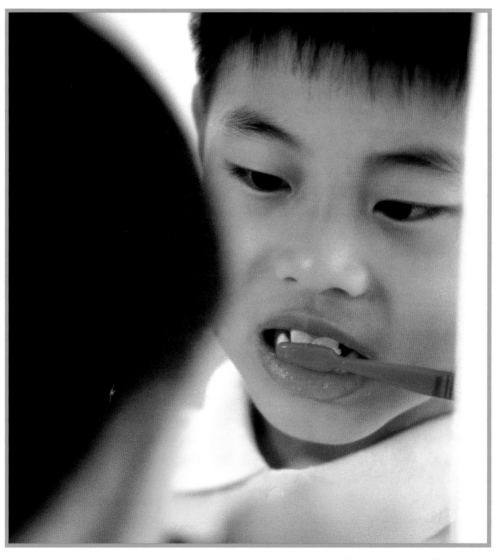

Brushing your teeth is one of the best ways for you to take care of yourself.

Brush Your Teeth!

The early Egyptians tried to clean their teeth. They rubbed crushed egg-shells and ash on their teeth with their fingers. Over the years, people also tried crushed shells and ground-up chalk or charcoal. Sometimes, they mixed these hard, grainy things with something sweet, such as honey.

Finally, in 1873, the Colgate Company created the first dental cream and sold it in a jar. The toothbrush was created in 1938 after the invention of nylon. Many years later, they began selling toothpaste in a tube. Now you can buy toothpaste in lots of cool flavors, colors, and packages. Today, brushing your teeth is really not so bad.

eating them just like they eat the sugar in your mouth. The result is a film in your mouth that tastes and smells bad.

Some people rinse their mouth with water as soon as they get up. Others brush their teeth, even before they eat breakfast. Getting rid of the bacteria makes the mouth feel fresh again.

CHAPTER FOUR

WHAT ARE SOME OTHER HYGIENE PROBLEMS?

Fungi are germs that love to grow in dark, damp

places. Mushrooms are a type of fungi. The

fungi that can make your body sick are

much smaller than mushrooms.

Do you like eating mushrooms? Mushrooms are one kind of fungi. (bottom)
With the help of a microscope, we can see what a common fungus
found in the lungs of humans and house pets looks like. (top)

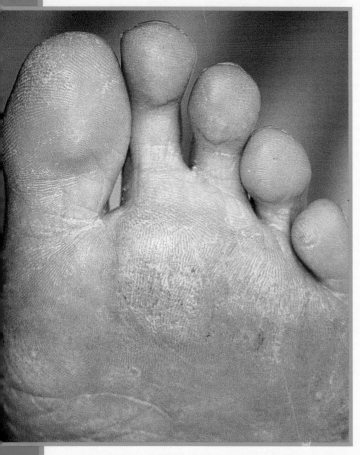

Athlete's foot is not fun to have. Protect yourself against it by not wearing dirty socks.

Sweaty shoes and socks are easy places for fungi to hide. They also like the wet floors found near swimming pools or dressing rooms. Fungi can grow on your skin and cause an itchy rash called athlete's foot. It usually grows between the toes or on the sole of the foot. Clean socks and feet are the best ways to prevent athlete's foot. Wearing rubber water shoes when you head to the swimming pool is also a good idea.

Did you know that small bugs can live on your skin? Head lice are tiny insects that can hide on the scalp of the head. They

If someone you know has lice, it's important to get yourself checked for them.

lay their eggs on shafts of the hair. They may be hard to see, but they are easy to feel. They make the scalp itch.

Often, several children in the same class will get lice. These little bugs are easily passed from one person to another. They can hide on combs, brushes, or even hats. That is why it is best not to borrow other people's hats or hair bands.

If you get head lice, you will need to wash your hair with a special shampoo. It will help get rid of the lice and their eggs. You will also need to clean everything that your head touched, like your pillow, sheets, combs, and hats. You do not want to pass lice on to your family.

This is a greatly magnified close-up view of a human head louse. (top)
Head lice are often passed from child to child at school. (bottom)

Children can also easily pass the germs that cause pinkeye to their family or friends. Pinkeye is an infection that causes the eyeball and lid to turn red. It also itches. When you rub your eyes, the germs move to your hands. Then it is easy to spread it to other students in the class.

A Bad Hair Day

Think you have trouble keeping your hair combed and clean? Try washing your hair in outer space! Without the help of gravity, it is hard to keep the water and shampoo on the hair.

Astronauts use a shampoo that does not have to be rinsed out of the hair. It was first made for people in the hospital who could not get out of bed.

Some women who have flown in space still want to use water to wash their hair. To do that in space, they have to squeeze just a little water at a time on their hair. If they use too much, the water drops will start floating away!

CHAPTER FIVE

HOW CAN YOU DEVELOP GOOD HYGIENE HABITS?

What is the best habit you can have to keep you healthy? Washing your hands with soap and water. It sounds simple, but many of us do not wash our hands the way we should.

Washing your hands is the most effective way to stop the spread of germs and to stay healthy.

Washing your hands is more than just rinsing and wiping them on a towel. Use warm water and soap. Rub your hands back and forth for at least 10 seconds to remove the germs. Be sure to get soap between your fingers and

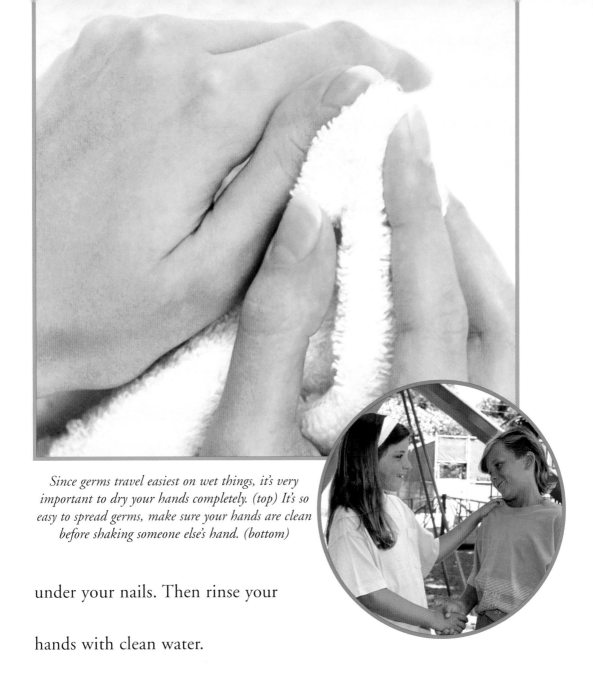

Since germs travel easiest on wet things, it's very important to dry your hands completely. (top) It's so easy to spread germs, make sure your hands are clean before shaking someone else's hand. (bottom)

under your nails. Then rinse your

hands with clean water.

Drying your hands is also part of the process. Germs travel

easiest on wet things. Damp hands can pass on more germs than

dry hands.

After playing outside, it's a good idea to wash your hands. Even if you can't see any dirt on them, chances are your hands are dirty and need to be washed.

Most children wash their hands only when they can see or feel

the dirt. Your hands need more help than that. Wash them before

you eat or cook in the kitchen. You should also wash after you use the bathroom. Remember that you cannot see the germs, but they are there.

Brushing your teeth two times a day is another habit that will keep you healthy. Be sure to brush the front and the back of your teeth. You also need to brush every tooth, even the ones at the back of your mouth.

Your great-grand-mother may not have used

When brushing your teeth, try to spend at least three minutes brushing. That way, you will know that your teeth are as clean as they can be.

a toothbrush when she cleaned her teeth. Before the toothbrush

was invented, many people used a stick to scrape their teeth.

Today, dentists say that you should use a soft toothbrush. That

way, you can clean your teeth without scratching the enamel.

These are just some of the products that people used to clean their teeth many years ago. They look a lot different than the toothbrush and tube of toothpaste that you use now, don't they?

While you are

taking care of your

mouth, do not

forget your

lips. The skin

on your lips can

get dry and crack or

peel. Then smiling and

eating can be painful.

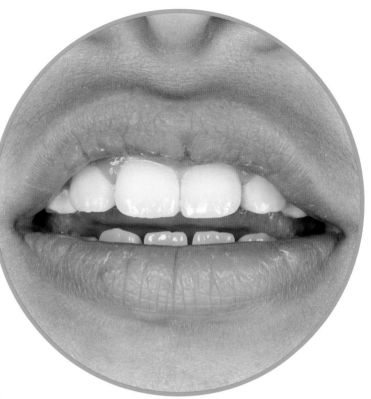

Having chapped lips can be painful. Lip balm will usually make them feel much better.

Putting cream on your lips will easily prevent chapped lips. In the

winter, you may need to do this several times a day.

Your skin needs extra care when you are going to play outside

—in the summer as well as in the winter. The sun can burn your

skin. Then your skin becomes bright red and very painful. Be sure to wear a hat and lots of **sunscreen.** Play in the shade

during the middle of the day, which is when the sun can cause the

most damage.

Sunburns can hurt a lot but they are easily preventable.
Make sure you put on protective sunscreen when playing outside on hot summer days.

Fight the chances that germs have to make you sick by practicing good hygiene.
That way, you'll have more time for doing the things you like to do.

Everyone gets sick sometimes. If you develop good habits, you
can keep lots of the germs from getting inside your body. Then
you will be playing instead of lying in bed feeling sick. How have
you fought germs today?

Glossary

enamel (i-NAM-uhl) Enamel is the hard outside layer of a tooth.

hygiene (HYE-jeen) Hygiene is the things people do to keep healthy and clean.

organisms (OR-guh-niz-uhmz) An organism is a living thing, such as a plant or an animal.

sunscreen sunscreen (SUHN-skreen) Sunscreen is a cream that helps protect the skin from the Sun's rays, which can burn the skin.

Questions and Answers about Hygiene

For how long should I brush my teeth? Try to brush your teeth for about three minutes. If that seems like a long time, turn on the radio and listen to a song while you brush.

What type of sunscreen should I wear? You should use a sunscreen with a sun protection factor (SPF) of 15 or higher.

Should I use antibacterial soap to wash my hands? Just washing with regular soap and warm water is enough to get rid of the bacteria on your hands.

Why shouldn't I bite my fingernails? Biting your nails allows the germs from your hands to move right into your mouth. Try to find ways to make yourself stop biting your nails. You'll be doing your body a favor!

Did You Know?

▸ About 2 square yards (1.7 square meters) of skin cover the body of an average adult. That is about the size of an American flag.

▸ You can get a sunburn even in the winter. Snow skiers wear sunscreen to protect their faces and necks from sunburn. The sun reflects off the snow and can cause a bad burn.

▸ Another name for bad breath is halitosis (ha-leh-TOW-sis).

▸ The number of germs on your hands doubles after you have been to the bathroom.

Would you shake this boy's hand?
Maybe after he washes his hands for about ten minutes and uses lots and lots of soap.

How to Learn More about Hygiene

At the Library
Brookes, Kate, and David Till (illustrator). *Wash Your Hands!*
New York: Smithmark, 1998.

Chandra, Deborah, and Madeleine Comora. *George Washington's Teeth.*
New York: Farrar Straus Giroux, 2003.

Miller, Debbie S., and Jon van Zyle (illustrator).
The Great Serum Race: Blazing the Iditarod Trail. New York: Walker & Co., 2002.

Schaefer, Valerie Lee, and Norm Bendell (illustrator). *The Care and Keeping of You.*
Middleton, Wis.: Pleasant Company Publications, 1998.

Vogel, Elizabeth. *Washing My Hands.* New York: PowerKids Press, 2001.

On the Web
Visit our home page for lots of links about personal hygiene:
http://www.childsworld.com/links.html

Note to Parents, Teachers, and Librarians: We routinely verify our
Web links to make sure they're safe, active sites—so encourage your
readers to check them out!

Through the Mail or by Phone
American Dental Association
211 East Chicago Avenue
Chicago, IL 60611
312/440-2500

Put on sunscreen every day and you won't have to worry about a painful burn.

Index

About the Author

Shirley Wimbish Gray has been a writer and educator for more than 25 years and has published more than a dozen nonfiction books for children. She also coordinates cancer education programs at the University of Arkansas for Medical Sciences and consults as a writer with scientists and physicians. She lives with her husband and two sons in Little Rock, Arkansas.